W9-CBX-467

NANCY TUMINELLY

Cool

RAW FOOD RECIPES

DELICIOUS & FUN FOODS WITHOUT COOKING

A Division of ABDO

ABDO
Publishing Company

visit us at www.abdopublishing.com

Printed in the United States of America, North Mankato, Minnesota
102012
012013

 PRINTED ON RECYCLED PAPER

Design and Production: Mighty Media, Inc.
Series Editor: Liz Salzmann
Photo Credits: to come

The following manufacturers/names appearing in this book are trademarks: Pyrex®, Ziploc®, Kitchen Aid®, Wholesome Sweeteners®, Blue Diamond®, MaraNatha®, Chatfield's®, Let's Do... Organic®, LouAna®, East Wind™, International Collection™, Osterizer®

Library of Congress Cataloging-in-Publication Data

Tuminelly, Nancy, 1952-
  Cool raw food recipes : delicious & fun foods without cooking / Nancy Tuminelly.
     pages cm. -- (Cool recipes for your health)
  Audience: 8-12
  Includes bibliographical references and index.
  ISBN 978-1-61783-584-1
1. Cooking (Natural foods)--Juvenile literature. 2. Raw foods--Juvenile literature. I. Title.
  TX741.T86 2013
  641.5'63--dc23
                              2012024002

TO ADULT HELPERS

This is your chance to introduce newcomers to the fun of cooking! As children learn to cook, they develop new skills, gain confidence, and make some delicious food.

These recipes are designed to help children cook fun and healthy dishes. They may need more adult assistance for some recipes than others. Be there to offer help and guidance when needed, but encourage them to do as much as they can on their own. Also encourage them to be creative by using the variations listed or trying their own ideas. Building creativity into the cooking process encourages children to think like real chefs.

Before getting started, establish rules for using the kitchen, cooking tools, and ingredients. It is important for children to have adult supervision when using sharp tools, the oven, or the stove.

Most of all, be there to cheer on your new chefs. Put on your apron and stand by. Watch and learn. Taste their creations. Praise their efforts. Enjoy the culinary adventure!

CONTENTS

RAW FOOD

People can eat some cooked food as part of a raw-food diet. But at least 75 percent of the food should be **unprocessed**.

LEARN MORE ABOUT COOKING RAW FOOD MEALS!

Following a raw diet means that you don't eat food that has been cooked or **processed**. That means eating fruits, vegetables, nuts, and seeds. These foods don't require heating. People choose to eat uncooked foods because of the health benefits. Some foods lose **vitamins** and **nutrients** when they are cooked.

There are a lot of foods for people who want to follow a raw-food diet. Try some of the raw-food recipes in this book!

When shopping, look for fresh ingredients. Be sure to avoid things that might be made with cooked or processed ingredients. Read the labels carefully.

Sometimes a recipe that includes cooked food will list raw **options** for those ingredients. Or, be creative and make up your own **variations**. Being a chef is all about using your imagination.

SAFETY FIRST!

Some recipes call for activities or ingredients that require caution. If you see these symbols, ask an adult for help!

Nuts - This recipe includes nuts. People who are allergic to nuts should not eat it.

Sharp - You need to use a sharp knife or cutting tool for this recipe. Ask an adult to help out.

THE BASICS

ASK PERMISSION

Before you cook, ask **permission** to use the kitchen, cooking tools, and ingredients. If you'd like to do something yourself, say so! If you would like help, ask for it!

BE NEAT AND CLEAN

- Start with clean hands, clean tools, and a clean work surface.
- Wear comfortable clothing.
- Tie back long hair and roll up your sleeves so they stay out of the food.

NO GERMS ALLOWED!

Some raw ingredients may have bacteria in them that can make you sick. After you handle raw foods, wash your hands, tools, and work surfaces with soap and water. Keep everything clean!

BE PREPARED

- Be organized. Knowing where everything is makes cooking easier!
- Read the directions all the way through before you start cooking.
- Set out all your ingredients before starting.

BE SMART, BE SAFE

- Never work alone in the kitchen.
- Ask an adult before using anything sharp, such as a knife, blender, or **grater**.

MEASURING

Many ingredients are measured by the cup, tablespoon, or teaspoon. Some ingredients are measured by weight in ounces or pounds. You can buy food by its weight too.

THE TOOL BOX

BAKING SHEET

BLENDER

CUTTING BOARD

FORK

GRATER

ICE POP TRAY

MEASURING CUPS

MEASURING SPOONS

MIXING BOWLS

MIXING SPOON

PAPER TOWELS

PLASTIC WRAP

The tools you will need for the recipes in this book are listed below. When a recipe says to use a tool you don't recognize, turn back to these pages to see what it looks like.

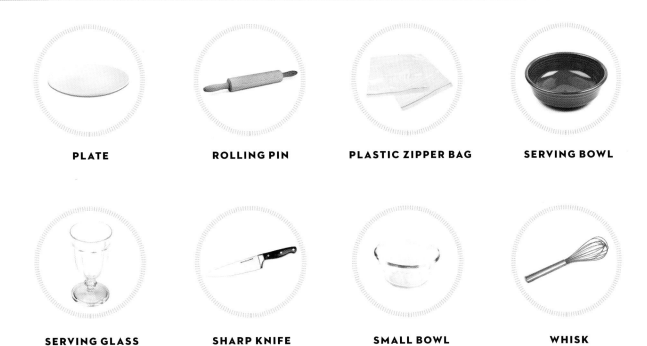

PLATE **ROLLING PIN** **PLASTIC ZIPPER BAG** **SERVING BOWL**

SERVING GLASS **SHARP KNIFE** **SMALL BOWL** **WHISK**

COOL INGREDIENTS

AGAVE NECTAR

ALMONDS
(MILK, BUTTER, NUTS)

AVOCADO

BANANAS

CAROB POWDER

CELERY

CILANTRO

CINNAMON

COCONUT &
COCONUT OIL

CORN KERNELS

CUCUMBER

CUMIN

DATES

FRESH
LEMON JUICE

GARLIC

ONIONS
(WHITE AND GREEN)

Many of these recipes call for basic ingredients such as salt and black pepper. Here are other ingredients needed for the recipes in this book.

HONEY

LETTUCE LEAVES

OIL
(SESAME & OLIVE)

ORANGE JUICE

ORANGE ZEST

PARSLEY

PEPPERS
(JALAPEÑO, RED BELL)

ROLLED OATS

SEA SALT

SNOW PEAS

SUN DRIED TOMATOES

TAHINI

VANILLA EXTRACT

VINEGAR
(BALSAMIC & APPLE CIDER)

WATERMELON

ZUCCHINI

COOKING TERMS

CHOP

Chop means to cut into small pieces.

COAT

Coat means to cover something with another ingredient or mixture.

DICE

Dice means to cut something into small squares with a knife.

GRATE

Grate means to shred something into small pieces using a **grater**.

MASH

Mash means to press down and smash food with a fork or potato masher.

Always wash fruit and vegetables well. Rinse them under cold water. Pat them dry with a **towel**. Then they won't slip when you cut them.

ROLL

Roll means to wrap something around itself into a tube.

SLICE

Slice means to cut food into pieces of the same thickness.

STIR

Stir means to mix ingredients together, usually with a large spoon.

TOSS

Toss means to turn ingredients over to coat them with seasonings.

WHISK

Whisk means to beat quickly by hand with a whisk or fork.

BANANA

BREAKFAST BLEND

makes 1 serving

INGREDIENTS

10 dates

¾ cup almonds

2 tablespoons coconut oil

1 tablespoon fresh raw coconut, grated

½ cup bananas, sliced

½ cup raw almond milk

TOOLS

measuring cups & spoons

serving bowls

paper towels

grater

blender

mixing spoon

sharp knife

cutting board

1 Put the dates in a bowl with 3 cups of water. Let them soak for 30 minutes. Pat them dry with a paper **towel**. Cut the pits out of the dates.

2 Put the dates, almonds, and coconut oil in a blender. Use the blend setting until the almonds are ground up. Hold the lid of the blender down while using it.

3 Put the coconut and bananas in a bowl. Add the date mixture. Stir.

4 Add the almond milk. Eat right away.

EVEN COOLER!

Add other fruits or nuts for extra flavor. Raspberries, blueberries, or even mangos all taste great!

R0120365390

CAROB SHAKE

makes 2 servings

INGREDIENTS

⅓ cup almonds

3 tablespoons carob powder

4 or 5 bananas, frozen and broken into chunks

¼ teaspoon vanilla extract

1 teaspoon honey

TOOLS

measuring cups & spoons

plastic zipper bag

rolling pin

blender

two serving glasses

16

STIR UP THIS SHAKE FOR A DELICIOUS DRINK!

1. Put the almonds in a plastic zipper bag. Use the rolling pin to crush them.

2. Put the pieces in the blender. Add the carob powder, bananas, vanilla, honey, and 1 cup water. Use the blend setting until the mixture is smooth. Hold the lid of the blender down while using it.

3. Put the mixture in the refrigerator for 30 minutes.

4. Pour the mixture into the serving glasses.

EVEN COOLER!

Use soy milk or a nut milk instead of water. See what you like best!

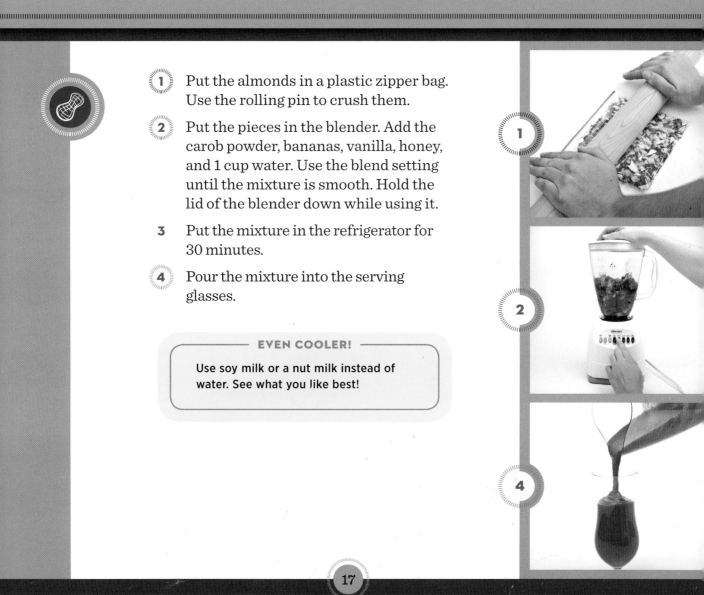

HUMMUS DIP

makes 1 cup

INGREDIENTS

1 zucchini

⅓ cup olive oil

⅓ cup tahini

3 cloves garlic

3 tablespoons lemon juice

¼ teaspoon sea salt

TOOLS

sharp knife

cutting board

measuring cups & spoons

blender

small bowl

1. Chop the zucchini into small pieces.

2. Put all the ingredients in the blender. Use the process setting until the mixture is smooth. Hold the lid of the blender down while using it.

3. Pour the mixture into a small bowl. Serve with veggies or crackers for dipping.

> **EVEN COOLER!**
>
> **Try cutting up some of your favorite veggies such as carrots or broccoli!**

VEGETABLE SALAD

makes 4 servings

INGREDIENTS

1 red bell pepper

¾ cup snow peas

3 green onions

2 celery stalks

½ cup fresh corn kernels

3 tablespoons chopped fresh cilantro

1 tablespoon balsamic vinegar

1 tablespoon apple cider vinegar

1 tablespoon agave nectar

1 tablespoon sesame oil

¼ teaspoon sea salt

TOOLS

sharp knife

cutting board

measuring cups & spoons

mixing bowls

mixing spoon

whisk

plastic wrap

1   Chop the pepper, snow peas, and onions into small pieces. Dice the celery.

2   Put the pepper, snow peas, onions, celery, corn, and cilantro in a large mixing bowl. Stir well.

3   Put the balsamic vinegar, apple cider vinegar, agave nectar, and sesame oil in a small mixing bowl. Whisk together.

4   Pour the vinegar mixture over the vegetables. Toss the salad. Sprinkle the sea salt over the top.

5   Cover the bowl with plastic wrap. Chill until ready to serve. Toss again before serving.

WATERMELON SOUP

makes 5 servings

INGREDIENTS

3 cups watermelon, chopped

1 cucumber, diced

1 red bell pepper, diced

1 small onion, chopped

1 whole jalapeño pepper

1 tablespoon olive oil

2 tablespoons lemon juice

2 tablespoons parsley, chopped

salt and black pepper

TOOLS

measuring cups & spoons

sharp knife

cutting board

blender

large mixing bowl

mixing spoon

plastic wrap

1. Put half the watermelon, cucumber, red pepper, and onion in the blender. Add the jalapeño, olive oil, and lemon juice. Use the puree setting until the mixture is smooth. Hold the lid of the blender down while using it.

2. Put the remaining watermelon, cucumber, red pepper, and onion in a large bowl. Add the parsley. Stir well.

3. Pour the blended mixture into the bowl. Stir well. Season with salt and pepper.

4. Cover the bowl with plastic wrap. Chill for 1 hour. Stir before serving.

LETTUCE WRAP

makes 8 servings

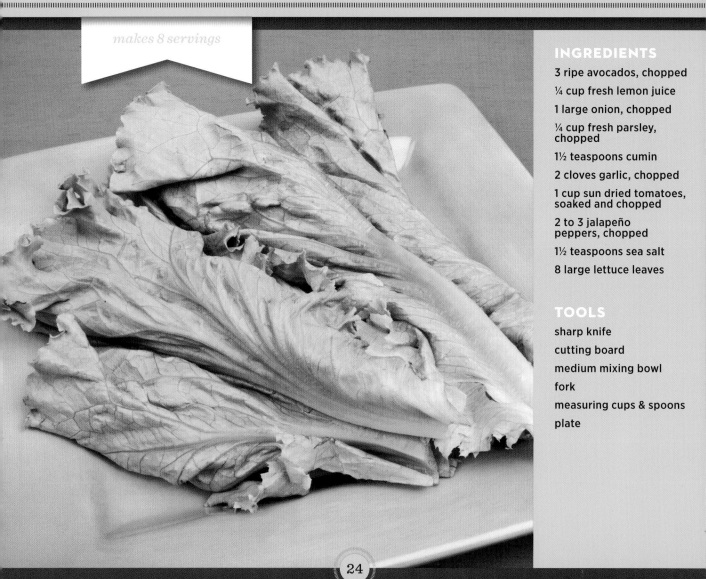

INGREDIENTS

3 ripe avocados, chopped

¼ cup fresh lemon juice

1 large onion, chopped

¼ cup fresh parsley, chopped

1½ teaspoons cumin

2 cloves garlic, chopped

1 cup sun dried tomatoes, soaked and chopped

2 to 3 jalapeño peppers, chopped

1½ teaspoons sea salt

8 large lettuce leaves

TOOLS

sharp knife

cutting board

medium mixing bowl

fork

measuring cups & spoons

plate

1. Put the avocado in a medium bowl. Mash it with a fork.

2. Add the lemon juice, onion, parsley, cumin, garlic, tomatoes, jalapeños, and sea salt. Stir well.

3. Lay a lettuce leaf flat on a plate. Put some of the avocado mixture on top. Roll up the lettuce leaf.

4. Repeat step 3 with the remaining lettuce leaves.

EVEN COOLER!

Try adding more jalapeños for an extra kick. Or chop up some other veggies such as carrots, broccoli, or cucumber.

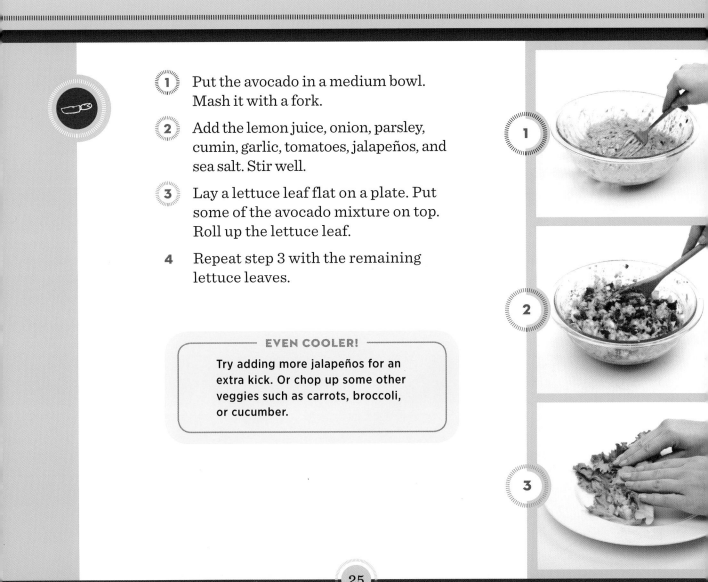

1

2

3

ORANGE ICE POP

makes 6 ice pops

INGREDIENTS

1 banana, mashed

1½ cups fresh orange juice

½ teaspoon orange zest

½ cup raw almond milk

2 tablespoons almond butter

1 teaspoon vanilla extract

TOOLS

measuring cups & spoons

mixing bowl

whisk

ice pop tray

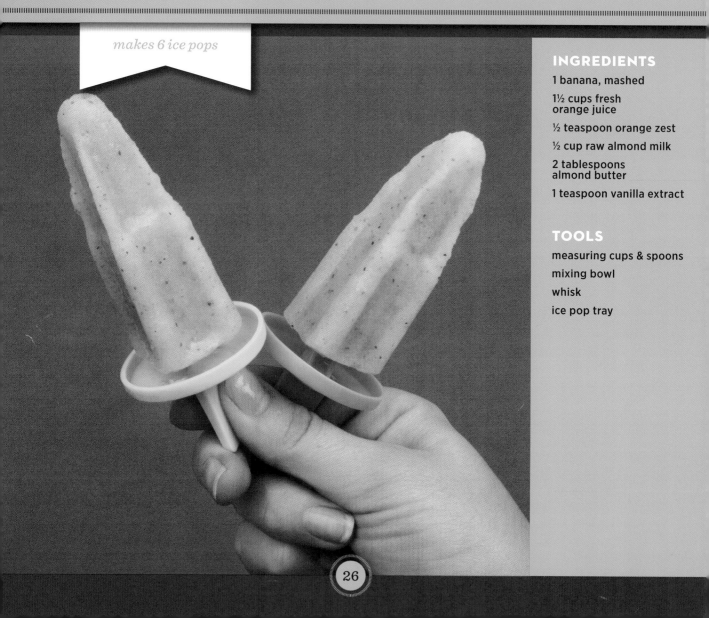

1. Put all of the ingredients in a mixing bowl.

2. Whisk the ingredients until evenly mixed.

3. Pour the mixture into the ice pop tray. Put the tray in the freezer for 2 hours.

4. Take the tray out of the freezer. Wait 5 minutes so the ice pops melt slightly. Gently wiggle the ice pop stick and slowly pull the ice pop out of the mold.

EVEN COOLER!

Try using other fruits such as blueberries, strawberries, mango, and watermelon.

FRIDGE COOKIES

makes 20 cookies

INGREDIENTS
2 cups almond butter

¾ cup honey

3½ cups rolled oats

3 tablespoons carob powder

1 tablespoon cinnamon

TOOLS
measuring cups & spoons

mixing bowls

mixing spoon

baking sheet

28

1 Put the almond butter and honey in a large mixing bowl. Stir well. Stir in 3 cups of oats.

2 Form the dough into balls. They should be about 1 inch wide.

3 Put the carob powder, cinnamon, and ½ cup oats in the small mixing bowl. Stir well. Coat each ball of dough with the carob mixture.

4 Place the balls of dough on a baking sheet. Chill for 1 hour before serving.

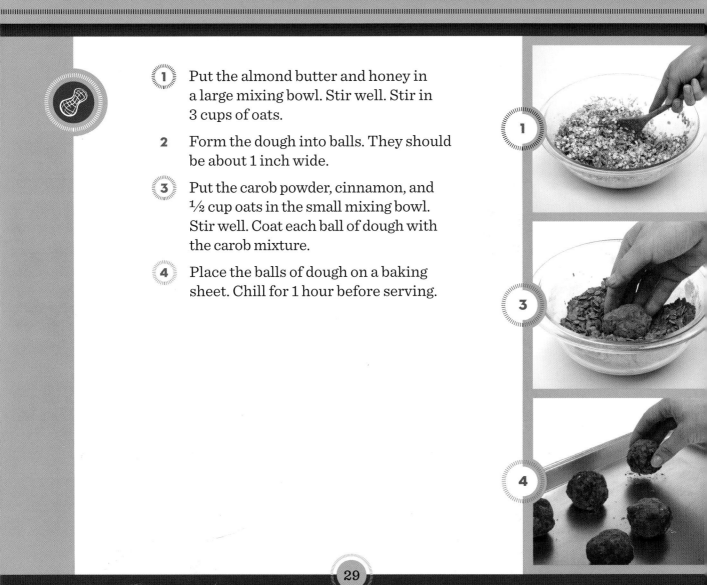

more about RAW FOOD LIFE

If you liked these dishes, look for other raw-food recipes. If you want or need to avoid eating cooked and **processed** foods, you have a lot of **options**!

Most food people usually eat has been cooked or processed in some way. Keep your kitchen stocked with healthy raw **alternatives.** Some great uncooked substitutes include fresh fruits, vegetables, and nuts.

Now you're ready to start making your own raw-food recipes. It takes creativity and planning. Check out different cookbooks. Look through the lists of ingredients. You'll be surprised how many dishes don't need to be cooked. Or you can come up with your own recipes or **variations**. The kitchen is calling!

A juicer is a great tool if you're on a raw-food diet. Put some of your favorite fruits in it to make a **refreshing** and **nutritious** drink!

GLOSSARY

ALTERNATIVE - something you can choose instead.

GRATER - a tool with rough-edged holes used to shred something into small pieces.

NUTRIENT - something that helps living things grow. Vitamins, minerals, and proteins are nutrients.

NUTRITIOUS - good for people to eat.

OPTION - something you can choose.

PERMISSION - when a person in charge says it's okay to do something.

PROCESSED FOOD - food that has been cooked, or had chemicals such as coloring, flavoring, or preservatives added to it.

REFRESHING - causing a feeling of new energy and strength.

TOWEL - a cloth or paper used for cleaning or drying.

VARIATION - a change in form, position, or condition.

VITAMIN - a substance needed for good health, found naturally in plants and meats.

WEB SITES

To learn more about cooking for your health, visit ABDO Publishing Company on the Internet at www.abdopublishing.com. Web sites about creative ways for kids to cook healthy food are featured on our Book Links page. These links are routinely monitored and updated to provide the most current information available.

INDEX